, & legibus canonū mor

habentes iure earū relaxationem.

xiiij imperfecta fanitas feu charitas morituri, neceffario fecum fert
magnū timorem, tātoꝗ maiorē, quāto minor fuerit ipfa.

xv Hic timor & horror, fatis eft, fe folo (ut alia taceam) facere pœ‑
nam purgatorij, cum fit proximus defperationis horrori.

xvj Videntur, infernus, purgatorium, cælum differre: ficut defpe‑
ratio, prope defperatio, fecuritas differunt.

xvij Neceffarium uidetur animabus in purgatorio ficut minui hor‑
rorem, ita augeri charitatem.

xviñ Nec probatū uidetur ullis, aut rationibus, aut fcripturis, ꝗ fint
extra ftatum meriti feu augendæ charitatis.

xix Nec hoc probatū effe uidetur, ꝗ fint de fua beatitudine certæ
& fecuræ, faltem oēs, licet nos certiffimi fimus.

xx Igitṝ Papa per remiffionē plenariā omniū pœnarū, non fimpli‑
citer omniū intelligit, fed a feipͦo tm̄modo impofitarū.

xxj Errant itaꝗ indulgentiarū prædicatores ij, qui dicunt per Pa‑
pæ indulgentias, hominē ab omni pœna folui & faluari.

xxij Quin nullam remittit animabus in purgatorio, quā in hac ui‑
ta debuiffent fecundum Canones foluere.

xxiij Si remiffio ulla omniū omnino pœnarū pōt alicui dari: certū
eft eam nō nifi perfectiffitnis. i. paucissimis dari.

xxiiij Falli ob id neceffe eft, maiorem partē populi: per indifferentē
illam & magnificam pœnæ folutæ promiffionem.

xxv Qualē poteftatē habet Papa ī purgatoriū gñaliter talē habet
ꝗlibet Epifcopus & curat⁹ in fua diocefi, & parochia fpāliter.

i Optime facit Papa, ꝗ nō poteftate clauis (quā nullam habet)
fed per modum fuffragij, dat animabus remiffionem.

ij Hominē prædicant, qui ftatim, ut iactus nūmus in ciftam tin‑
nierit, euolare dicunt animam.

iij Certū eft nūmo in ciftam tinniente, augeri quæftum & auari‑
ciam poffe: fuffragiū aūt ecclefiæ eft in arbitrio dei folius.

iiij Quis fcit fi omnes animæ in purgatorio uelint redimi, ficut de
fancto Seuerino & pafchali factum narratur?

v Nullus fecurus eft de ueritate fuæ contritionis: multo minus

a ij

"We are beggars, this is true."

Luther's last written words, 1546

minedition

English editions published 2016 by Michael Neugebauer Publishing Ltd., Hong Kong

Text copyright © 2016 Géraldine Elschner
Translated by Kathryn Bishop, English text.
Bilder:
© AKG-images for the cover image and the image of the 4th coating and for pages 5, 6 - 7, 10, 11, 15, 17, 18, 25, 28 & 30 - 31
© Artothek for pages 19 & 27
© Bridgeman for pages 2 - 3, 8, 9, 13, 16, 21, 22 - 23, 24, 26 & 29
Rights arranged with "minedition" Rights and Licensing AG, Zurich, Switzerland.

Michael Neugebauer Publishing Ltd., Unit 23, 7F, Kowloon Bay Industrial Centre, 15 Wang Hoi Road, Kowloon Bay, Hong Kong.
Phone +852 2807 1711, e-mail: info@minedition.com
This edition was printed in June 2016 at L.Rex Printing Co Ltd.
3/F., Blue Box Factory Building, 25 Hing Wo Street, Tin Wan, Aberdeen, Hong Kong, China
Typesetting in Silentium Pro designed by Jovica Veljovic
Library of Congress Cataloging-in-Publication Data available upon request.

ISBN 978-988-8341-34-4
10 9 8 7 6 5 4 3 2 1 First Impression

For more information please visit our website: www.minedition.com

Martin Luther
"Here I stand..."

Told and Designed by Géraldine Elschner
Translated by Kathryn Bishop

minedition

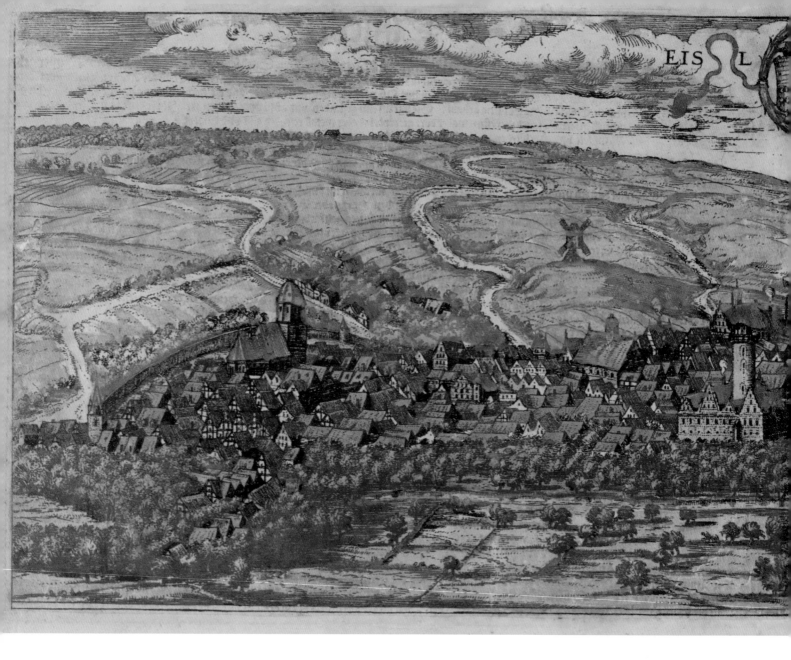

ere is where it all began.
In 1483, in the small German town of Eisleben,
Hans and Margarethe Luder interrupted
their journey to Mansfeld. It was time.
Their son Martin was born on November 10th.
Luder was their name—only later would
they be called Luther.

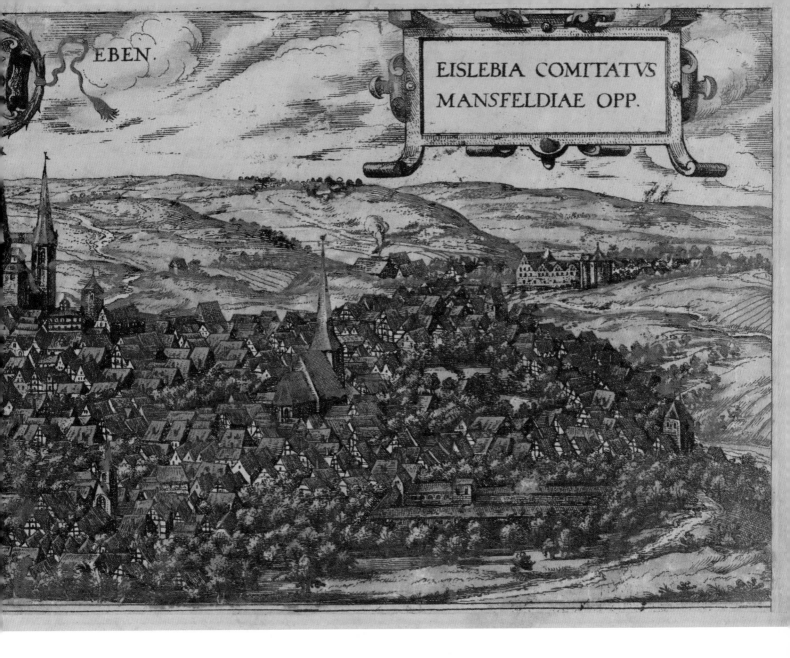

EBEN.

EISLEBIA COMITATVS
MANSFELDIAE OPP.

Hans Luder was a farmer's son who found
work in copper mining.
There was money to be made,
and the family would continue to grow.
Margarethe worked hard to provide for the family.

Martin liked to sing; he was cheerful,
clever, and studied diligently. His parents were
proud of him. He was to become a lawyer
and would prosper.
But in July 1505 Martin was caught in a terrible
storm. Lightning struck near him, knocking him
to the ground.
He was terrified and cried out in agony to St. Anne,
"Help me and I will become a monk."

Two weeks later he did just that. He became
a monk in the religious order of the Augustians,
and gave up his law education for a life of prayer,
fasting, and religious study.
His father was furious.

AETHERNA IPSE SVAE MENTIS SIMVLACHRA LVTHERVS
EXPRIMIT·AT VVLTVS CERA LVCAE OCCIDVOS·

·M·D·XX·

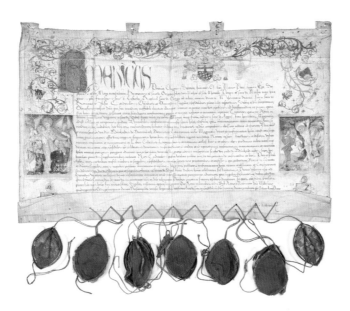

Fast. Pray. Work.
This was his day, and it began at 3:00 a.m. with the first of hourly prayers.

Martin became a priest and began studying again, becoming a professor of theology at the University of Wittenberg.

However, there was much in the Church he didn't like.
On a trip to Rome, for example, he discovered that people with money could buy forgiveness for their sins in order to guarantee a place in heaven.
Instead of feeling regret, they only needed to purchase a so-called "indulgence." This was a way to buy God's pardon, and the money was used to build the new St. Peter's Basilica.

Martin was horrified.
Buying a place in heaven was not acceptable.
He loved truth and openly said that though he often doubted, he was never in despair.
His God was "a mighty fortress," one that gave him strength and courage.
He had to do something.
So Luther wrote a list of his complaints, known as theses, to his bishop–95 short paragraphs in all.

It is believed that he had even nailed the 95 theses to the door of the All Saint's Church in Wittenberg.
Nailed with a big hammer, hung like a placard for all to see–the noise must have resounded all over the city.

It began...
"Out of love for the truth and the desire to bring it to light..."

The people read and were amazed.
Who was the man who dared to write such things, who stood alone against Rome, against the church, and against the Pope?

"A rebel!"
"A heretic!"

Martin was summoned to Rome by the Pope to answer charges of heresy.
Did he respond to the summons? No!
Would he recant? Never!

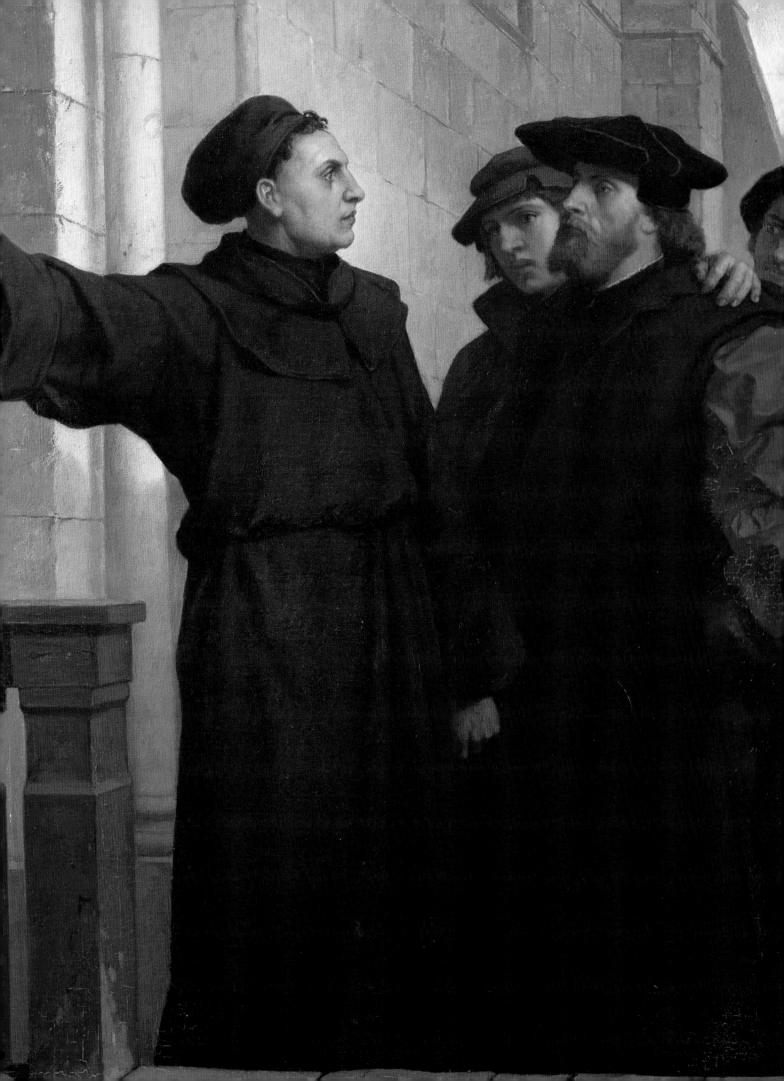

he summons was soon followed by a letter from the Pope threatening to ban him from the church.

What did Martin do?

He publicly burned the letter at the gates of Wittenberg.

He wanted no quarrel, but he didn't want to retract his theses either, not before the Pope, and not before the Emperor. After an official assembly in Worms, an edict deprived Martin of all his civil rights and even threatened his life.

It is said that Luther responded, "Here I stand...I can do no other."

In 1521, the break was complete, both with Rome and with the Empire.

Luther fled to Wartburg Castle, a lonely refuge deep in the Thuringian Forest where he could remain safe.

artin hid away, disguised as "Junker Jörg" (Young Lord George).

Although he liked the nature, the trees, and "the area of the birds" as he called the fortress on top of the mountain, the loneliness of exile was hard on him.

Convinced that life and the love of God was a gift, fear still plagued him.

He supposedly even threw his inkwell at Satan, whom he believed to see at night.

"From Heaven above to earth, I come..."

To fight back against the evil spirits he prayed and sang, wrote songs and began to translate the Bible into German.

He worked, day and night.

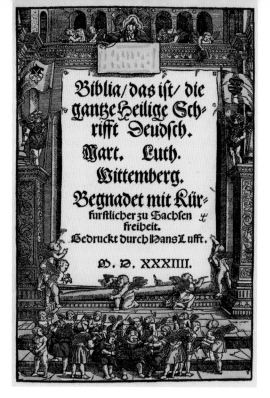

After three months his translation of the New Testament was complete.

It took twelve years to finish the Old Testament, but in 1534, this most influential of German Bibles appeared.

Up to this point reading the Bible was only possible for those who could read Latin, Hebrew or Greek.

Luther wanted everyone to be able to read and understand the Bible.

The common people needed vibrant language, rich in imagery–and this was how he transcribed it.

Johannes Gutenberg's new printing press in Mainz helped speed the journey of Luther's words and his Bible far and wide.

utside the castle of Wartburg, the reform had started to take hold.

A new church arose, a Protestant church, following the ideas of Luther and other like-minded reformers. But the church was forbidden in some areas, and its followers were persecuted.

Luther felt the fighting had gone too far.
There should be no violence, no war.
And so he returned to Wittenberg and tried to bring order.
He traveled the country, preaching, putting his teachings in writing and...

he married Katharina Bora, a former nun who had been forced to flee her convent. Whether nun, monk or priest, all should be allowed to marry. This was one of Luther's reforms.

Six children, "the finest game birds" grew up in his house, three girls and three boys.
He liked making music with them. For Martin, music was "the best of God's gifts."
At his large table sat not only the family but relatives, students, friends, and travelers.
As master of the house, his table talk was well known, even the harsh words.
They ate well–very well, and they spoke of many things, not only about God.

But as Luther aged, he told his students, "I am weak, I can do no more."

A trip to Eisleben would be his last.
Here he was born, and here he died on February 18, 1546. His circle of life was complete.

The house where he died is today one of the Luther memorials.

As the "cradle of the Reformation," it was added, along with his birth house, to the list of **UNESCO** World Heritage sites in 1996, where a new era of religious history began.

Even after the death of the reformer, his ideas lived on, spreading from Germany and Switzerland throughout other European countries where long religious wars raged.

Lutheranism and its offshoots were carried around the world, from Asia to South America, from Canada to Australia.

And as ships reached the coast of North America emigrants founded the first communities, many with Protestant churches.

In 1934,
a Baptist preacher from the United States, a Mr. King,
traveled to Europe.
He visited the places of the Reformation in Germany
and was impressed.
What new thoughts this reformer had had and what
courage!
Upon his return to the United States, he changed
his name and that of his eldest son Michael,
to Martin Luther.

His son, Martin Luther King Jr., protested
racial segregation in America and received
the Nobel Peace Prize in 1964 for his
commitment to equal rights.

"I have a dream..." he said.
Like the 95 theses nailed to the church door, the
dream of a free and just world resounded then
as today.
The name of Martin Luther lives on, now
doubled, and continues to travel across borders.

OUT OF T